GET OUT ALIVE!

ESCAPE FROM TALONS OF TERROR

Julie K. Lundgren

Published in the United States of America by Cherry Lake Publishing Group
Ann Arbor, Michigan
www.cherrylakepublishing.com

Reading Adviser: Beth Walker Gambro, MS, Ed., Reading Consultant, Yorkville, IL

Photo Credits:
© Zdendyska33/Shutterstock, cover, contents page (owl); © Geoffrey Kuchera/Shutterstock cover (skunks), page 13 (top), page 14; © klyaksun/Shutterstock (graphic on cover and throughout book); © Alexander Wong/Shutterstock, page 4; © Annette Shaff/Shutterstock, page 5 (owl), wingspan owl from Shutterstock, © VALUA VITALY/Shutterstock, page 5 boy; © yongsheng chen/Shutterstock, page 6; © jdross75/Shutterstock, page 7; © owls page 8 and 9 (top) from Shutterstock, © Gary C. Tognoni/Shutterstock, page 9 (bottom); © Rebecca Shaughnessy/Shutterstock, page 10; © Ronnie Howard/Shutterstock, page 11 (owls), owl pellet from Shutterstock;© Hayley Crews/Shutterstock, page 12-13, © Hayley Crews/Shutterstock page 13 (top); © AZ Outdoor Photography/Shutterstock, page 15 (top), © Holly Kuchera/Shutterstock, page 15 (bottom), © Lisa Fischer/Shutterstock, page 15 WOW graphic; © klyaksun/Shutterstock, page 16 green spray; © Nynke van Holten/Shutterstock, page 17, page 19 (top), and page 23; © Agnieszka Bacal/Shutterstock, page 18; © Cynthia Kidwell/Shutterstock, page 19 (bottom); © Kalebjeppson125/Shutterstock, page 20; © Martin Prochazkacz/Shutterstock, page 21 (top), © Michal Ninger/Shutterstock, pages 21 and 22 (bottom); Page 22 © muratart/Shutterstock, (top);

Produced for Cherry Lake Publishing by bluedooreducation.com

Copyright © 2026 by Cherry Lake Publishing Group

All rights reserved. No part of this book may be reproduced or utilized in any form or by any means without written permission from the publisher.

Library of Congress Cataloging-in-Publication Data has been filed and is available at catalog.loc.gov.

Printed in the United States of America

Note from Publisher: Websites change regularly, and their future contents are outside of our control. Supervise children when conducting any recommended online searches for extended learning opportunities.

About the Author

Julie K. Lundgren grew up in northern Minnesota near Lake Superior. She delighted in picking berries, finding cool rocks, and trekking in the woods. She still does! Julie's interest in nature science led her to a degree in biology. She adores her family, her sweet cat, and Adventure Days

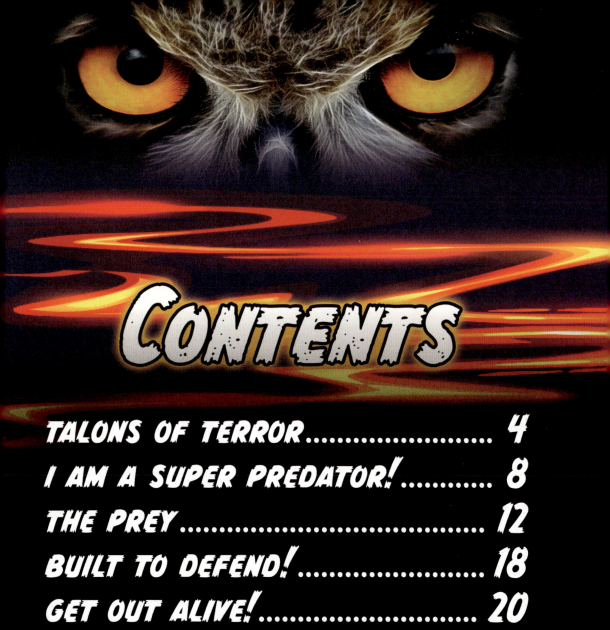

Contents

TALONS OF TERROR.......................... **4**
I AM A SUPER PREDATOR!............ **8**
THE PREY... **12**
BUILT TO DEFEND!......................... **18**
GET OUT ALIVE!............................... **20**
FIND OUT MORE............................. **24**
GLOSSARY.. **24**
INDEX.. **24**

Talons of Terror

Who, who, whooo strikes terror from the night sky?

My gray, brown, and tan feathers help me hide. I use my ears and eyes to find and kill prey.

GREAT HORNED OWLS HAVE SOFT CAMO FEATHERS FOR WARMTH AND STEALTH.

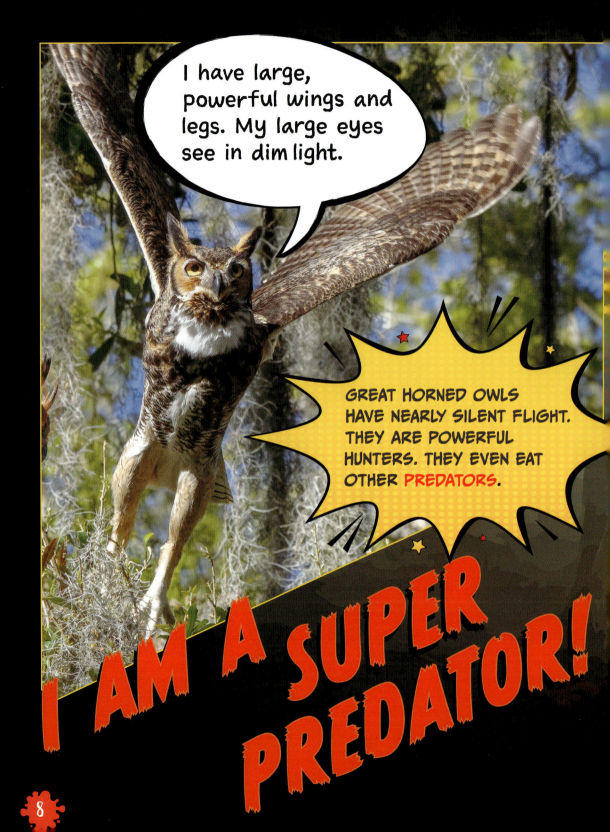

SENSITIVE EARS UNDER THE DARK FACE FEATHERS CAN HEAR THE TINIEST SOUNDS.

TOUGH, BUMPY SKIN AND LONG, SHARP TALONS HELP GRIP SLIPPERY, OR BLOODY, PREY.

9

Great horned owls live in wild places and in cities. They spy prey from a tree or roof, somewhere they can see all around.

THE PREY

Striped skunks roam at dawn and dusk. They dig for grubs. They hunt mice and insects.

Striped skunks nest in burrows or hollow logs. In spring, they have two to ten babies. Baby skunks are called kits.

Humans smell skunks waaaaaay before we see them. Striped skunks stink all the time. But they stink more when they spray their oily butt perfume, called musk, at attackers.

SKUNKS CAN BLAST THEIR STINKY SPRAY AS FAR AS 12 FEET (3.65 METERS).

PEE-YEW!

BUILT TO DEFEND!

ALL SKUNKS WARN BY STAMPING THEIR FEET, RAISING THEIR TAILS, AND AIMING THEIR BUTTS AT PREDATORS. SOMETIMES THEY DO HANDSTANDS!

"If I raise my tail, watch out! Stink glands near the base of my tail blast my stinky spray."

Skunks have good hearing and a sensitive nose to detect danger. They have sharp teeth and claws.

GET OUT ALIVE!

The night is nearly over. A skunk comes out of its burrow to look for food. It digs and sniffs. An owl hears the rustle of leaves and grasses.

A SKUNK CAN WEIGH UP TO THREE TIMES AS MUCH AS AN ADULT GREAT HORNED OWL.

Find Out More

Books

Barnes, Rachel. *Great Horned Owls*, Minnetonka, MN: Bellwether Media, 2024

Nichols, Catherine. *Smelly Skunks*, New York, NY: Bearport Publishing, 2019

Websites

Search these online sources with an adult:

Great Horned Owls | National Geographic Kids

Skunks | Britannica

Glossary

burrows (BUR-ohz) underground homes for some animals

camo (KAM-oh) short for camouflage, the colors and patterns that help animals hide

owlets (OW-lets) baby owls, until they leave the nest

predators (PREH-duh-terz) animals that hunt and kill other animals, usually by stealth

prey (PRAY) animals hunted and eaten by other animals

regurgitated (ree-GUR-juh-tay-tihd) brought back up and emptied or spat from the mouth

rustle (RUS-uhl) a soft crinkling or scratching sound, as when dry leaves rub together

stealth (STELTH) quiet sneakiness

talons (TAL-uhnz) very sharp claws on birds of prey used for catching and killing prey

Index

beak 5
crow(s) 22, 23
ears 6, 7, 9
eyes 6, 8, 17
kits 14, 15

owlets 11
prey 6, 7, 9, 10, 11, 21
spray 16, 17, 19, 22
talons 5, 7, 9
warning 22